Contents

Any words appearing in the text in bold, **like this**, are explained in the Glossary.

What is bendy?

This toy snake is bendy. You can move its body into many different shapes. Which letter does it make here? (Answer on page 31.)

Some things have to bend to work properly. This girl is trying on a belt. She bends it round her waist and through the buckle.

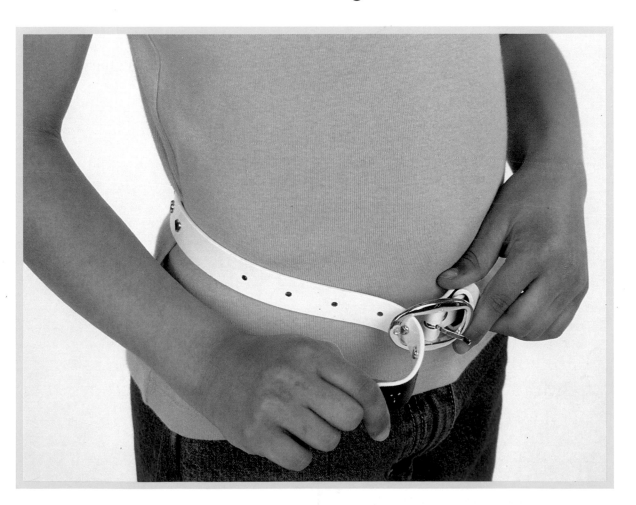

How bendy?

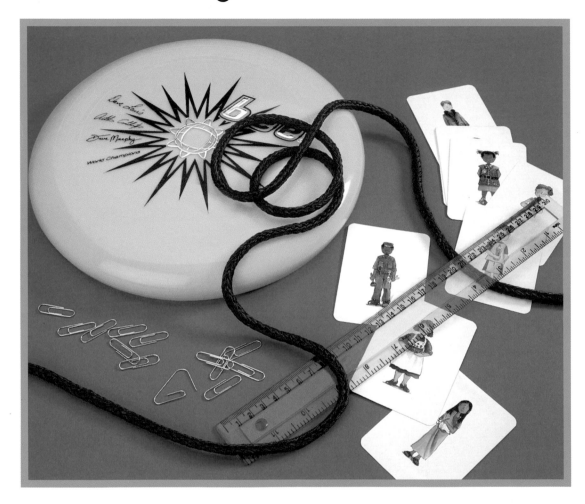

Some things bend more than other things. The playing cards bend more than the ruler. But the rope is the bendiest thing of all in the picture.

These children want to find out whose shoe is the bendiest. They bend each shoe without breaking it. Which shoe is the bendiest? (Answer on page 31.)

What is rigid?

This xylophone is rigid. This means that you cannot change its shape by bending it. However much you push or pull it, it stays the same shape.

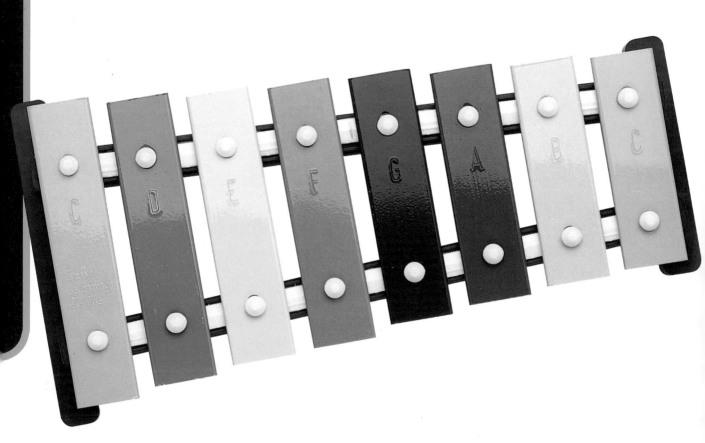

The pan and the plate are both rigid.
This is just as well! They would be
useless if they bent when something
heavy was put on them.

How rigid?

The wooden ruler is quite rigid. It
keeps its shape unless you bend it.
Even then it only bends a little bit.

The **screwdriver** is more rigid than the wooden ruler. But the most rigid thing in the photo is the tile. The tile does not bend at all.

Plastic

Some plastic is bendy. This coat is made of a kind of plastic. Being bendy makes it easier to put on and to move around in.

This plastic **hosepipe** is very bendy.
It can be wound into a circle when
it is not being used. But the plastic
watering can is rigid.

Wheels

Bicycle wheels have **rubber** tyres.
Rubber is strong but bendy. It bends
as you go over a bump in the path.

Bicycle wheels have a rigid **rim** and rigid **spokes**. The rim and the spokes hold the wheels in shape. What shape are the rims in this picture? (Answer on page 31.)

Shoes

Shoes bend as you walk. This allows you to bend your foot. The bottom of a shoe is made of strong plastic or **leather**.

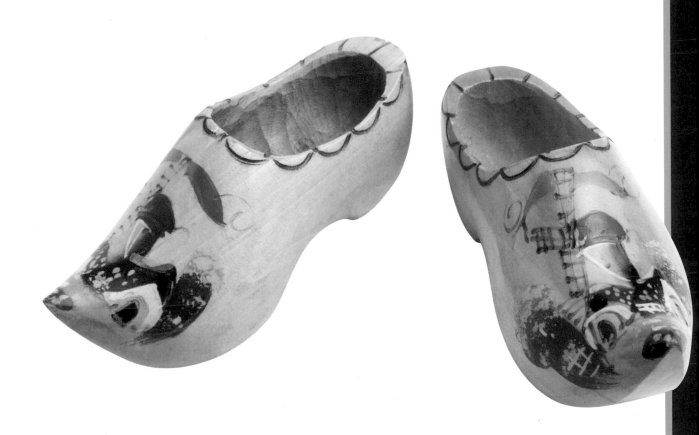

These **clogs** are made of wood.
The wood is rigid and does not
bend as you walk. It is not very
easy to walk in clogs!

Paper and cardboard

A sheet of paper is very bendy. It can be rolled into a tube or folded several times. When you unroll the sheet it becomes flat again.

Cardboard is thicker than paper. It is also more rigid than paper. It does not bend easily. Thick cardboard is used to make strong, rigid boxes.

Thick and thin

It is easier to bend something that
is thin than something that is thick.
These thick **girders** will not bend
easily. They make a rigid steel frame.

These paperclips are made of steel, just like the thick girders. But the paperclips are thin. This makes them easy to bend.

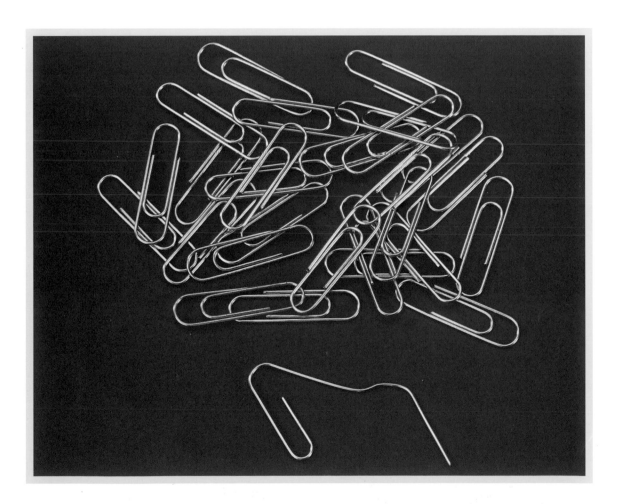

Bending and breaking

Most bendy things can only bend so far. Then they break. This woman is bending the stick until it breaks into two pieces.

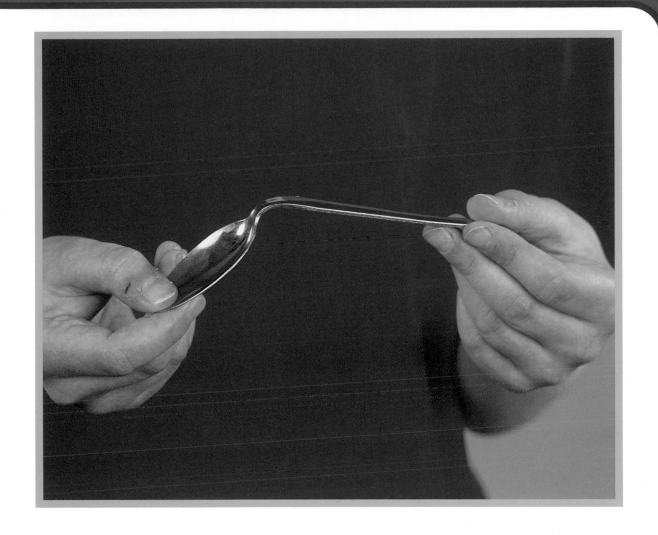

Some things bend and break by mistake. This spoon is bent. If it is bent back and forwards over and over again, the metal will become weaker. Eventually, it will snap in two.

Wood can bend

Sometimes wood can bend. This cat's basket is made out of wooden twigs. The twigs are bent and twisted together.

Trees bend when they are blown by strong winds. These palm trees are being bent by the strong winds of a **hurricane**. Bending stops the trees from being blown over.

China is brittle

Rigid things do not bend, but they break.
Some rigid things are **brittle**, like these
china cups and saucers. This means that
they crack or break easily.

Plates, mugs, bowls and ornaments are often made of china. Be careful not to drop china! If it is dropped, it may break into many pieces.

Other brittle materials

Glass is even more **brittle** than **china**, especially if it is thin. These glasses are **fragile**. They are made of very fine glass that breaks easily.

Stones and bricks are brittle too. But they are so thick they do not break easily. This worker is using a **sledgehammer** to break up the stone.

Glossary

brittle easy to break into pieces
china material that is often used to make plates, bowls, cups and vases
clog a shoe with a bottom made of wood
fragile easy to break or to damage
girder a thick piece of steel used to hold up a building
hosepipe a long tube that carries water from a tap
hurricane a storm that includes very strong wind and very heavy rain
leather material made from the skin of a cow or other animal
rim edge
rubber bendy material made from the juice of the rubber tree
screwdriver tool used to screw nails into wood
sledgehammer a big, heavy hammer
spokes set of thin rods that join the **rim** of a wheel to its centre

Answers

page 4
The snake makes the shape of the letter S.

page 7
The girl has the bendiest shoe.

page 15
Each wheel rim makes the shape of a circle.

Index

Look
After Yourself

Get Some Rest!

Angela Royston

Heinemann

www.heinemann.co.uk/library
Visit our website to find out more information about **Heinemann Library** books.

To order:
 Phone 44 (0) 1865 888066
 Send a fax to 44 (0) 1865 314091
 Visit the Heinemann Bookshop at www.heinemann.co.uk/library to browse our catalogue and order online.

First published in Great Britain by Heinemann Library, Halley Court, Jordan Hill, Oxford OX2 8EJ, part of Harcourt Education.
Heinemann is a registered trademark of Harcourt Education Ltd.

Editorial: Sarah Eason and Kathy Peltan
Design: Dave Oakley, Arnos Design
Picture Research: Helen Reilly, Arnos Design
Production: Edward Moore

Originated by Dot Gradations Ltd
Printed and bound in Hong Kong and China by South China

ISBN 0 431 18021 0 (hardback)
07 06 05 04 03
10 9 8 7 6 5 4 3 2 1

ISBN 0 431 18031 8 (paperback)
08 07 06 05 04
10 9 8 7 6 5 4 3 2 1

British Library Cataloguing in Publication Data
Royston, Angela
Get some rest. – (Look after yourself)
1.Rest – Juvenile literature
I.Title
613.7'9

A full catalogue record for this book is available from the British Library.

Acknowledgements
The publishers would like to thank the following for permission to reproduce photographs: Bubbles p.**5** (Lucy Tizard) p.**9** (Frans Rombout), p.**25** (Ian West); Getty Images p.**11** (Peter Hince), p.**13** (David Roth), p.**16** White Packert); Last Resort p.**24** (Jo Makin); Photodisc pp.**10**, **21**, **26**; Powerstock pp.**4**, **8**; Science Photo Library p.**14** (Gaillard, Jerrican), p.**20** (Mark Clarke); Trevor Clifford pp.**6**, **7**, **15**, **18**, **19**, **22**, **23**, **27**; Trip p.**12** (S. Grant), p.**17** (S. Grant).

Cover photograph reproduced with permission of SuperStock/Kwame Zikomo.

The publishers would like to thank David Wright for his assistance in the preparation of this book.

Every effort has been made to contact copyright holders of any material reproduced in this book. Any omissions will be rectified in subsequent printings if notice is given to the publishers.